Original title:
Snapdragon Solace

Copyright © 2025 Creative Arts Management OÜ
All rights reserved.

Author: Lucas Harrington
ISBN HARDBACK: 978-1-80566-712-4
ISBN PAPERBACK: 978-1-80566-997-5

Beneath the Blooming Veil

In a garden bright with color,
Bees are buzzing like a motor.
Petals laugh, they whirl and dance,
While the gardener breaks a glance.

The carrots in their silly hats,
Frolic with the friendly cats.
Sunflowers bend to share a joke,
As daisies giggle, oh what a folk!

With twinkling stars above the buds,
The earth's alive, yet full of thuds.
A butterfly lost in a spin,
Bounces off a cheeky spin.

So come and join the flower's jest,
Where laughter blooms, you'll feel the best.
In this place where joy prevails,
Life's a banquet, full of tales.

Echoes in the Floral Breeze

Underneath the sky so blue,
Flowers share a laugh or two.
Honeybees wear tiny shoes,
While snails play cards, win or lose.

Tulips sport their fanciest gowns,
Chasing away the grumpy frowns.
Rosy petals burst with glee,
Telling tales of bumblebees.

Whimsical fronds wave hello,
As breezes join the flower show.
Marigolds with their bright smiles,
Swirling, spinning for miles and miles.

So come, partake in this delightful game,
As petals wink and dance, not the same.
In this world of colorful cheer,
Each moment's laughter, crystal clear.

A Haven in Lavender Light

In a field of lavender hue,
Laughter floats on morning dew.
Sassy critters plan their pranks,
While flowers gather for their thanks.

Daffodils crack jokes on the sly,
As butterflies giggle and fly high.
The sun dips low with a mischievous grin,
Whispering secrets, it's sure to win.

Caught in a breeze, scents wander wide,
While dainty blooms sit side by side.
Their petals flutter with pleasure and ease,
Tickling the air like a gentle tease.

So come explore this playful plight,
Where every petal brings delight.
A carnival of colors and mirth,
A joyful wonder, a colorful birth.

Secrets of the Wildflower Grove

Hidden deep where wild blooms play,
A silly rabbit hops all day.
With daisies whispering something sweet,
The wise old owl takes a seat.

Foxgloves gossip, petals swirl,
As prankster frogs give tails a twirl.
Ladybugs wear polka-dotz with flair,
While butterflies attend, a dazzling affair.

Squirrels dance atop the stalks,
Mimicking the buzzing talks.
In this grove of giggle and cheer,
Every bloom and creature holds a dear.

So wander in this raucous glade,
Where friendships bloom, never fade.
With vibrant colors leaping about,
Laughter echoes; that's what it's about!

Resilience in Vibrant Tints

In the garden of colors, laughter blooms,
Petals wear smiles, casting away glooms.
A squirrel in shades of tangerine rush,
Trips over roots with a comical hush.

Butterflies joke as they flit through air,
Like clowns in disguise, without a care.
Flora laughs softly, whispering cheer,
A saxophone's giggle that only we hear.

The Heart of the Botanical Realm

Bumbles buzz by, their dance is a jest,
In this leafy domain, they flit with a zest.
Tulips exchange tales, bold and absurd,
While daisies chime in, laughing unheard.

Roots play peek-a-boo beneath the ground,
Tickling the soil, with giggles abound.
Nature's ensemble, a quirky delight,
Where laughter grows tall, and nothing's contrite.

Wisteria Dreams

Wisteria hangs low, tying knots in the breeze,
Whispering secrets to the bumblebees.
A jester-like vine twists and turns with flair,
Drapes itself elegantly, as if not a care.

In this purple realm, the shadows play tag,
A dance of delight, not a reason to brag.
Petals tumble down, giggling in sight,
They twirl in the air, oh what a funny flight!

Embrace of the Lush Green

Amidst the embrace where the ferns like to sway,
Laughter spills over in a bright green ballet.
A turtle grins wide, moves slowly in time,
While the grasshopper dances, crafting its rhyme.

Leaves rustle softly, sharing a prank,
Nature in motion, an uproarious prank.
The globe spins a yarn in this emerald glow,
With humor enfolding, like a bright leafy bow.

Petals and Peace

In a garden full of cheer,
Petals giggle, shedding fear.
Bees wear tiny, buzzing hats,
While butterflies play with the cats.

A sunflower tells a silly joke,
As poppies laugh and gently poke.
The daisies dance to a funny tune,
While shadows skip beneath the moon.

Solace Among the Leaves

Among the leaves, a squirrel prances,
Wearing socks, it takes its chances.
With acorns tossed like silly dreams,
It creates unexpected schemes.

A chipmunk trips on a fallen twig,
Laughs it off, doing a jig.
Branches whisper with delight,
While the crickets chirp goodnight.

The Stillness of Thorns

Thorns stand tall, quite proud and sly,
Pretending to be tough, oh my!
But when the wind starts to tease,
They wiggle and bend with utmost ease.

In a prickly patch, laughter reigns,
As roses play their funny games.
With humor sharp as any blade,
They bloom in jest, unafraid.

Elixirs of the Earth

The earth brews potions, oh so rare,
With giggles bubbling in the air.
A daisy stirs with a crooked spoon,
While mushrooms dance to a cartoon tune.

In muddy puddles, frogs conspire,
For a splashy jump, they do require.
With every drop, joy flows and swirls,
As nature crafts its funny pearls.

A Tapestry of Floral Whispers

Petals giggle in the breeze,
As bees dance like they're on skis.
Colors clash in playful shout,
A garden party—come check it out!

Sunlight drips like honey sweet,
Daisies kick in rhythmic feet.
Every blossom joins the jest,
Nature's laughter, truly blessed!

Resting in Floral Embrace

Bumblebees in cozy beds,
Whisper secrets in flower heads.
Tulips wear a silly frown,
While daisies twirl their skirts around.

Gentle vines tickle your toes,
Wind-caught giggles, nobody knows.
Petals wink with carefree flair,
A floral hug beyond compare!

Threads of Lavender and Hope

Lavender laughs with a cheeky grin,
While bees buzz tales of where they've been.
The violets tease the shyest bloom,
In this cheerful flower room.

Forget-me-nots play hide and seek,
While roses whisper, "Oh, so chic!"
Daffodils wearing hats of fun,
In the sunshine, all have won!

Nature's Gentle Refrain

Sunflowers nod like they're in a trance,
While petals perform their silly dance.
The wind cracks jokes that twirl and spin,
Each leafy friend cannot help but grin.

Garlands twine in dizzy delight,
As nature chuckles day and night.
With every bloom, a laugh is near,
A fragrant joy, forever dear!

Lullabies of the Flourishing Grove

In the grove where giggles play,
Bumblebees dance without delay.
Trees chuckle in the gentle breeze,
While squirrels hold their stand-up tease.

Flowers wear their brightest grin,
Tickling vines just to fit in.
The sun winks with its golden ray,
As shadows join the silly fray.

The Stillness of Nature's Muse

The brook hums tunes of silly bliss,
Frogs croak out their crooner's kiss.
Crickets play their night-time jam,
While owls laugh at the whole grand slam.

With mossy hats and dandelion crowns,
The critters tell their jesting towns.
Each stillness holds a secret rhyme,
Nature's giggle through all of time.

A Tapestry of Fragrant Memories

Petals blush in vibrant hues,
As daisies nod with gentle cues.
The breeze whirls tales of yesterday,
Where laughter lingered, come what may.

Scents of mischief fill the air,
Rosemary's wink and thyme's soft stare.
Lavender dreams with cheeky flair,
Entwined in life's sweet, funny care.

Where the Wildflowers Weep

Wildflowers giggle in the rain,
Tickled petals feel no pain.
Raindrops play a slapstick show,
While roots catch laughter from below.

In fields where whimsy takes a stroll,
Each blossom plays its funny role.
Nature's tears can't dampen fun,
Just a child's chat with a big, bright sun.

A Portrait in Flower-Cast Light

In gardens where silliness blooms,
Petals dance, dispelling glooms.
Grass tickles toes under the sun,
Nature's laughter, oh what fun!

Bees wearing hats, buzzing with cheer,
Whispering secrets only we hear.
A flower's wiggle, a bright pink shoe,
Plant folks strut, oh what a view!

Morning glories stretching high,
Swaying, winking at the sky.
A daisy trip, a clumsy twist,
In this taste of floral mist!

With every bloom, joy wraps around,
In petal parties, laughter is found.
A jester's cap on a sunflower's head,
In this colorful stage, we are led!

Breaths of Harmony

Whimsical winds play tunes so bright,
In leafy laughter, spirits take flight.
A lilac chuckles, a rose tries to sing,
In the garden, happiness is king!

The crocus dons a vibrant cape,
Room for mischief, no need to escape.
Insects tango, all glowing and bold,
As pollen giggles, its stories unfold.

A tulip teases, "What's in your cup?"
The sun spills nectar as we cheer up.
Forget the worries, the world can wait,
In this patch of joy, life is first-rate!

Robins plot characters in their play,
The petals nodding, "What do they say?"
In each tiny seed, a jest waits to bloom,
In this garden, we're never in gloom!

The Spirit of the Flowerbed

In flower beds, a charade of cheer,
Colors bouncing, nothing to fear.
A daffodil pirate, with a cheeky grin,
Commanding the daisies, "Let the fun begin!"

Chirping crickets, they tap dance away,
While lilies chortle around in a sway.
The tulips whisper of the plans they make,
For mischief and laughter, look at the stake!

Sunflower scouts with binoculars wide,
Searching for giggles they can't hide.
A carnival here, with scents that tickle,
In this flowerbed, life never gets fickle!

Giggles abound by the soft petals' grace,
Every corner a bright, happy space.
In jest, they bloom, and in joy, they spread,
The spirit of laughter dances ahead!

Tranquil Tendrils of Life

In a tangle of leaves, jokes intertwine,
Vines twist in laughter, oh how they shine.
A garden of whimsy where fables delight,
Stories of mischief bloom day and night!

Fluffy clouds join the flower parade,
As bees wear tuxedos, perfectly made.
Dandelions giggle as they take flight,
In the embrace of this cheerful light.

Caterpillars boast of their vibrant stripes,
While laughing with butterflies, plotting their gripes.
The marigolds tease with their bright orange flair,
In a theatre of blossoms, life's never bare!

In tranquil tendrils, humor flows free,
Each snap of a stem, a new chance to see.
In this joyful realm, where laughter does thrive,
We greet the world with glee, oh so alive!

Solitude Among the Blossoms

In a garden where laughter plays,
Petals giggle in sunlit rays.
Bees wear ties, buzzing in style,
While flowers dance and laugh for a while.

A butterfly flaunts its vibrant flair,
Winks at the daisies, they giggle and stare.
Worms in tuxedos wiggle with glee,
A grand floral ball, come dance with me!

Caterpillars sip on dew drops of cheer,
They'll munch on greens, their favorite sphere.
Amidst the blooms, there's no gloomy frown,
Even the soil wears a joyful crown.

So come, dear friend, let humor unfold,
In this garden of laughter, and blossoms bold.
With a chuckle and smile, let's lift up the day,
For in flowery humor, we'll always play.

The Language of the Sun-Kissed Earth

The daisies converse in giggles and sighs,
While sunbeams cast goofy shadows and ties.
A dandelion joins in, a fluffball of cheer,
Declares itself king, with regality clear.

In the soil, the jokes are sprouting with zest,
Each seedling is teasing, trying its best.
With roots that entangle, they plot and they scheme,
In this playful domain, nothing's as it seems.

Ants line up, wearing shoes made of leaves,
With tiny umbrellas, for rain that deceives.
Together they march, on a whimsical quest,
Seeking sweet nectar, the very best fest.

The sun winks down, with a smile so bright,
While rainbows decide to join in the plight.
With humor and joy, the earth spins around,
In this sun-kissed domain, pure laughter is found.

A Refuge in Floral Whispers

Among the petals, stories unfold,
Of comical blooms, courageous and bold.
A rose tells a tale, of thorns and delight,
While violets giggle, their colors so bright.

In this refuge of laughter, a lilac will chime,
Singing a melody, perfect in time.
The sage cracks a joke, with wisdom to share,
While marigolds chuckle, their fragrance in air.

The sunflowers sway, with heads full of sun,
Claiming that no weed can ever outrun.
With roots interwoven, they share in their jest,
In this floral hideaway, we're all truly blessed.

So let us retreat, where the blossoms are free,
Where the whispers of flowers invite you and me.
In this garden of giggles, with humor so sweet,
Life blossoms together, in joy we meet.

Hues of Serenity and Grace

In the meadow where colors collide,
Sunflowers smile with petals so wide.
They whisper in hues, both vibrant and bright,
Creating a canvas of pure delight.

The lilies pose, with styles so refined,
While a rogue daffodil's humor's unconfined.
A gentle breeze carries laughter along,
Nature's own symphony, cheerful and strong.

The violets gossip, in violet attire,
Sharing sweet secrets, that never expire.
The colors unite, in a dance full of zest,
Bringing warmth to the heart, oh what a fest!

With every shade painting joy in the air,
This floral tapestry, beyond compare.
In all of their grace, they offer us cheer,
In the hues of their laughter, we gather near.

Reflections in a Blooming Prism

In the garden where colors play,
Petals giggle in a cheerful sway.
Leaves gossip secrets that tickle the air,
The sun blushes bright, unaware of its flair.

Buzzing bees wear tiny hats,
Dancing around like quirky acrobats.
Worms tell tales of their underground digs,
While butterflies flaunt their radiant wigs.

Each flower grins, a silent jest,
A posy parade that never takes rest.
Bouncing colors like a clown on a spree,
Nature laughs loudly, so wild and free.

So tiptoe lightly through blossoming cheer,
Laughter echoing, crystal clear.
In this sunny realm of whimsy and hue,
The world giggles back at you.

A Chronicle of Hidden Beauties

In shadows where shy blooms reside,
Pansies peek with a wink, full of pride.
Tulips hold court like old, jolly dames,
Whispering tales, playing little games.

Roses wear crowns with thorns for the jest,
While daisies cheer in their pastel best.
A lilac giggles, too ticklish to stand,
As violets plot mischief, oh so unplanned.

Secret adventures lie just out of sight,
In the clamor of colors, what pure delight!
Petals narrate their comical schemes,
While the breeze carries smirks and dreams.

So stroll through this plot of vibrant disguise,
Among curious blooms that sing and surprise.
Each turn reveals a squeaky new line,
In this garden of humor where sunflowers shine.

The Serenity of Flowering Souls

In a whirl of petals, laughter rings,
Cheerful blossoms with many bright wings.
Sunflowers nod like grinning old friends,
While tulips crack jokes that never quite end.

Daisies play hide and seek with the breeze,
While pansies jest, 'We're the real elites!'
A rose blushes, but let's not misstate,
With every soft poke, it can't help but celebrate.

Frolicking flora in joyous array,
With each sway and spin, they dance and play.
In harmony rich, they tell their own tale,
Of pastimes and laughter, through green, verdant vale.

So lean in and listen to this floral glee,
Where laughter blooms wild, so carefree.
In every corner, a giggle unspools,
Reflecting sweet fun in the garden's jewels.

Beneath the Veil of Verdant Dreams

Beneath green canopies where chuckles reside,
Whimsical wonders of nature abide.
Petals twirl with a giggling flair,
While secretive creatures peek with a stare.

Frogs wear spectacles, croaking in rhyme,
While squirrels lug acorns as toys in their climb.
The moon chuckles softly, watching it unfold,
As flowers tell tales that never grow old.

Breezes swing by with a tickle and tease,
Whispering nonsense through overhanging leaves.
A rose throws a party for all its chums,
While daisies tumble with giggles and hums.

So dance through this patch of whimsy and cheer,
Where nature's laughter is tasty and clear.
In the embrace of blooms where fun is supreme,
Join in the rollicking, beneath the lush dream.

The Gentle Heart of Wildflowers

In the field where daisies sway,
Bumblebees dance and laugh all day.
With petals bright, they prance around,
Tickling toes upon the ground.

The violets gossip, oh what a scene,
Sharing secrets of grass so green.
The sun is a jester, casting its glow,
As butterflies giggle, putting on a show.

A daffodil hears a joke from a rose,
It chuckles so hard, the laughter just flows.
With each little breeze, more laughter ignites,
In this happy patch, all worries take flight.

As shadows grow long, the giggles remain,
In nature's own circus, there's no need for pain.
With petals for seats, and clouds for the stage,
The wildflower's heart is joyfully sage.

Echoes of the Garden Path

Strolling along the meandering trail,
The hedgehogs and rabbits spin tales without fail.
With a hop and a skip, they jump in the air,
On this lively path, every creature's laid bare.

The roses are snickering, sweet fragrant laugh,
While the ferns unfurl, writing their own gaff.
Sun's shining bright, as squirrels make a dash,
Over pots of tokens, like some crazy stash.

The daisies, they wink, with a tease in their style,
As snails widely grin, plotting mischief awhile.
The grasshoppers joke, with banter so light,
On this garden path, the spirits take flight.

When twilight creeps in, oh what a delight,
The whispers of giggles fill the air with their bite.
In this enchanted yard, joy echoes anew,
With every sweet whisper, the laughter just grew.

Blossoms of Calm

In the quiet grove where the soft winds sigh,
A chubby little squirrel dashes by.
The flowers stand still, mouths open with glee,
As daisies declare, "Hey, come play with me!"

The lilacs chuckle, tickling the boughs,
While butterflies flit, taking playful bows.
Here shadows whisper tales of the breeze,
And caterpillars giggle, just as they please.

A gentle bee hums its own silly tune,
While the sun peeks out, a jolly cartoon.
There's laughter in petals, a soft, soothing balm,
Creating a space with an aura so calm.

As dusk settles down, the crickets all dance,
On this stage of green, they take their own chance.
With blossoms of calm, the world starts to fade,
And the joy of the night wraps us in a cascade.

Colors of a Still Heart

In a painting of hues where the laughter begins,
Each petal's a brushstroke, where whimsy spins.
The yellows and reds prancing in glee,
Turn every plain day into a grand spree.

The lavender giggles, pool-side comfy embrace,
As the oranges twirl in a dazzling race.
The violets are blushing, caught in the glint,
Of the sun's golden rays, oh what a hint!

Among all this color, a surprise we can find,
A jester named pollen, so playful, so kind.
It tickles the noses of creatures who roam,
In this garden of joy, we all feel at home.

When twilight drapes softly, the colors unite,
As laughter and dreams cradle us tight.
In a world filled with colors, oh what a treat,
With a still heart so full, our lives are complete.

The Heartbeat of Living Color

In gardens bright with hues so loud,
The flowers dance, they laugh, they crowd.
A bee with style buzzes around,
In this wild disco, joy is found.

With every petal, a wink and nod,
Nature's pranksters beneath the sod.
Silly bugs in a wacky race,
Chasing shadows, a comical chase.

The sun sneers down, a golden grin,
While butterflies join in, spin, and spin.
A party where the colors meld,
In the heart of cheer, joy is held.

So laugh a little, don't take it hard,
Life's a carnival, stand on guard.
With blooms that giggle, flutter, and sway,
The heartbeat of color is here to stay.

Blossoms at Dusk

When twilight falls, and day takes flight,
The blooms awake with pure delight.
They whisper secrets, oh-so-fine,
In shades of purple, pink, and wine.

A dandelion, with cheeky flair,
Makes wishes float through evening air.
While tulips giggle, their petals prim,
As fireflies twinkle, dance, and skim.

With shadows stretching, they all conspire,
To throw a bash, oh, how they inspire!
Gather the gnomes, and fill the tea,
For blossoms at dusk are wild and free.

So take a stroll, and join the fun,
Where flowers party with everyone.
At the close of day, with laughter bright,
The blossoms shine in the soft moonlight.

The Hushed Soliloquy of Petals

In quiet corners, the petals speak,
With whispers soft, so mild, so meek.
They share their tales, both bold and shy,
About the clouds that float on by.

A sunflower sings of the sun's embrace,
While daisies giggle in their white lace.
Roses, in blush, share secrets sweet,
Of love's own game, a comical feat.

Their whispers weave through the evening air,
A laughter that's gentle, beyond compare.
With every breeze, they dance and sway,
In the hush of dusk, where dreams play.

So listen close to their blooming cheer,
For petals know more than they appear.
In their quietude, find joy unfurled,
A softness that brightens the whole wide world.

Nurtured by Nature's Brush

With strokes of green, the artist dreams,
Painting blooms with laughter's gleams.
A tickled tulip giggles bright,
While violets shyly take flight.

In gardens where the sun bestows,
The bloom brigade puts on their shows.
Each petal tipped with humor's art,
In colors bright, they share their heart.

A bloom parade with hats in style,
Winks to bees with the cutest smile.
With every blush, each fragrant sigh,
Nature laughs and waves goodbye.

So come and join this floral glee,
Where laughter dances, wild and free.
Nurtured by nature's quirky touch,
Life's hilarious blooms mean so much!

Whimsical Colors in Dappled Light

In the garden, colors play,
Dancing shadows come to stay.
Bumblebees in silly flight,
Buzzing jokes, what a delight!

Petals flutter, bright and bold,
Secrets in their folds unfold.
Sunshine giggles through the leaves,
While laughter tickles, sweet reprieves.

Frogs in hats and dancing snails,
Whispering through botanical tales.
A cupcake tree, a lemon pie,
In this world, oh my, oh my!

Unicorns with polka dots,
Playing hopscotch, not just plots.
Every corner, whimsy shines,
In this space where joy entwines.

Tranquility Nurtured at Twilight

As dusk begins to paint the sky,
Fireflies flicker, oh my, oh my!
A sleepy cat with dreams of cheese,
Scratching at the evening breeze.

Twirling leaves in evening's glow,
A dance party with roots in tow.
Crickets laugh, their tunes divine,
Nature's sitcom, quite benign.

Stars peer down with twinkling eyes,
Chasing moths as sweet surprise.
Whispers float on cooling air,
Balloons of laughter everywhere!

In this moment, peace does bloom,
Underneath the silver moon.
With joy swelling in our hearts,
Nature's hug, where fun imparts.

A Nest of Flowers

A cozy spot with hues so bright,
Flowers chirp in pure delight.
Daisies wearing tiny hats,
Complain about the looking cats.

Butterflies in goofy grace,
Waltzing 'round, they find their place.
Softly giggling, petals sway,
In this joyful, floral play.

A dandelion bursts with pride,
"I'm a lion," it confides.
Roses chuckle, soft and sweet,
Baking cakes for all to eat.

In this nest of blooms we find,
A patchwork quilt, the best designed.
Colorful quirks in every seam,
Lively laughter, nature's dream.

Souls Intertwined in Blooming Harmony

Two flowers swaying side by side,
In the breeze, they confide.
A sunflower whispers, "You're my best!"
While tulips wear a flowered vest.

Bumblebees buzz a happy tune,
Discord not in nature's boon.
Every petal sings a song,
In this garden, they belong.

Roses meeting with their kin,
Hold a party, let's begin!
Violets joke about the sun,
"Watch us twinkle, isn't fun?"

In this harmony, laughter flows,
A tapestry of joy that grows.
Nature's bond, a perfect rhyme,
A wacky dance throughout all time.

Tranquil Echoes in Bloom

In gardens lush where giggles play,
A flower sneezes, blooms go astray.
Petals whirl like a joyful kite,
The bees all buzz, what a silly sight!

With colors bright, they dance in glee,
A tulip trips on a bumblebee.
A daisy chuckles, a rose starts to sing,
Nature's laughter is a marvelous thing!

Sunbeams tickle the leaves on high,
The wind joins in, a playful sigh.
Worms wear hats, what a foolish charm,
In this green haven, there's naught to harm!

So come, dear friend, let's join this show,
Amidst the blooms where silliness flows.
For in this space, we all can be,
As wild as flowers, carefree and free!

A Serenade of Colors

With paintbrush strokes, the petals sway,
A giggling flower bids the sun to play.
Green grass stretches, tickling toes,
As butterflies plot their silly shows!

A marigold talks to a cheeky ant,
"Tell me the joke that you overheard, plant!"
They chuckle and laugh, a quip to share,
As daffodils twirl, swinging in the air!

Bees wear tuxedos, oh what a sight,
Sipping sweet nectar with pure delight.
The lilacs giggle, such fragrant fun,
Their scent is a prank that's never quite done!

In this riot of colors, nothing's amiss,
Even the bugs join in for a bliss.
So stand in awe; let your heart take flight,
In this world of laughter, everything's right!

Heartstrings of the Wildflower

A wildflower whispers to the breeze,
"Is that sun or just another tease?"
With roots entwined, they chuckle low,
Sharing secrets only they know!

A bumblebee dons a tiny crown,
Buzzing around, never wearing a frown.
With every bloom, a story is spun,
Of playful pranks and crooked fun!

Carrots giggle, the rabbits hop,
Silly tales that never stop.
Nature's orchestra plays a tune,
Full of mischief from dawn to moon!

So take a stroll where wildflowers lie,
Join their revelry under the sky.
For in their laughter, joy will grow,
In a dance with nature, let your heart flow!

Echoes of the Quiet Meadow

In the meadow where whispers reside,
A clover makes a merry slide.
"Careful!" cries out a nearby toad,
As daisies tumble, light and bold!

Chirping birds banter from tree to tree,
"Did you hear of the squirrel's latest spree?"
With laughter ringing in the soft air,
Nature's jokes are beyond compare!

The wind plays tricks on a tall oak tree,
Its leaves quiver at the comedy spree.
Beneath the sunshine, the meadows glow,
Where even the shadows join in the show!

So stroll through the greens, let the giggles out,
As the world around you turns about.
For in this space of humor's embrace,
We find life's joy in nature's grace!

Blooms that Tell a Story

In gardens where the daisies dance,
They whisper secrets, take a chance.
With floppy hats and giggles bright,
They spin their tales from day to night.

The roses roll their eyes in jest,
While violets chuckle, feeling blessed.
Each bloom is filled with laughter sweet,
In this wild world, the flowers meet.

A sunflower grins, tall and proud,
While daisies shout, 'Let's be loud!'
Petals poof like fluffy clouds,
As nature laughs in flower crowds.

So, take a stroll through this bouquet,
Let blooms reveal their funny play.
In every hue and every shape,
They gossip wildly; oh, what a drape!

Petal-Soft Serenade

Roses croon in colors bright,
Swaying gently, pure delight.
A lilac blushes, then it beams,
As daisies swoon in springtime dreams.

The tulips tiptoe in a line,
While buttercups just sip on wine.
A dandelion starts to twirl,
With each soft breeze, it gives a whirl.

As violets laugh, oh what a sight,
They tell the grass, 'Come join the fight!'
With petals soft, they sway and sway,
Gathering all the joy of May.

So listen close, dear friend of mine,
To nature's jest, a soft design.
In every bloom, a joke so sly,
Floral fun beneath the sky.

A Realm Beneath the Green Canopy

Underneath the leafy shade,
Where giggles of the flowers played.
The ferns gossip, what a fuss,
While petals roll, just making a bus.

A clover crew, with luck to share,
Tells tall tales to the passing air.
Whimsical weeds in a playful brawl,
Bring laughter echoing through them all.

Moss cushions the feet of blooms,
Adventures hide in their dusty rooms.
Each bud a joker, fresh and spry,
Beneath the canopy, oh my, oh my!

So join the frolic, let's not delay,
In this realm where flowers play.
In every inch of shade and sun,
Life's a garden, let's have fun!

The Sanctuary of Wild Blooms

In the sanctuary where blooms collide,
Petals bounce with joyful pride.
The poppies giggle, line by line,
As dandelions chase after brine.

Orchids wink with fancy flair,
While pansies prance without a care.
Their laughter paints the morning air,
Creating magic everywhere.

The daisies put on quite a show,
Juggling dew drops in a row.
A tulip plays the trumpet loud,
As bees hum softly, oh so proud.

So look around, embrace the thrill,
In this wild place, your heart will fill.
A sanctuary of humor and glee,
Where every bloom is wild and free!

Swaying with the Fragrance of Peace

In the garden, bees are buzzing bright,
Bump into flowers, they take flight.
Slipping on petals, oh what a sight,
Nature's dance makes everything feel right.

The daisies gossip, having a chat,
While the wind joins in wearing a hat.
Sunbeams tickle, oh look at that!
Even the grass is doing a spat.

Wandering gnomes wave with a grin,
Waving at clouds that float and spin.
A chorus of laughter, where to begin?
In this merry land, joy's a sure win.

So come and sway with the scents of cheer,
Join in the fun, don't you fear!
Nature's laughter, oh so near,
In the fragrant fields, let's persevere!

An Ode to the Earth's Beauty

Oh, the rolling hills with their grassy sprawl,
A trampoline for squirrels, oh what a ball!
The leaves whisper secrets, through trees they call,
Nature's humor, charming us all.

Rivers giggle, skipping with glee,
While frogs wear crowns, oh so haughty!
Sunflowers stand tall, sipping their tea,
Nature's court jesters, don't you agree?

A fruity aroma wafts through the air,
Apples in line, showing off flair.
Pine cones tumble down, not a care,
In this beauty, laughter's everywhere!

Join the chorus, let spirits soar,
Earth's kaleidoscope, we all adore.
In every crack, there's a joke galore,
In this lively world, oh, to explore!

Respite in Nature's Cocoon

In a cozy nook beneath a grand tree,
I found a snail drinking chai, fancy and free.
Butterflies prance, where could they be?
Nature's comedy, a sight of jubilee.

Ladybugs gossip, perched on a leaf,
Discussing the day with joy and relief.
A hedgehog snorts, oh what a belief,
That nature's antics bring laughter, no grief.

Clouds wear sweaters, fluffy and light,
Silly shadows dancing, a curious sight.
A picnic of joy, from morning till night,
In this cocoon, all feels just right.

So take a seat, embrace the delight,
In this charming nook, laughter's in sight.
Nature's silliness, pure and bright,
In her warm circle, we all unite!

Feathers of Flora

Petals like feathers, fluttering around,
Bouncing like bunnies, never profound.
Each flower a dancer, none are quite bound,
In this floral circus, fun's always found.

A clumsy bumblebee stumbles and falls,
Sipping sweet nectar, heed not the calls.
With a wiggle and jive, it bounces off walls,
In the garden's mirth, everyone enthralls.

Worms in a conga line wiggly and spry,
Telling the daisies they're aiming to fly.
Mice in the grass playing peek-a-boo sly,
In this lively scene, laughter's the high.

So frolic with blossoms, let your heart soar,
Join in the laughter, there's always more.
In the garden of giggles, forever explore,
With feathers of flora, life we adore!

Resilience in the Garden's Heart

In every bloom, a joke is sown,
Roots tangled like a cellphone.
The daisies giggle, the roses pout,
'What's this mess? We're all about!'

A gopher pokes his nose so spry,
Winks at the tulips, 'Oh me, oh my!'
Laughter echoes from leaf to leaf,
Even the weeds find joy in grief.

The sun breaks through with a goofy grin,
While fruits and veggies sing, 'Let's begin!'
With veggies dancing, carrots in tow,
Who knew a garden could steal the show?

And when it rains, they wear their hats,
Splashing water like silly cats.
In nature's chaos, humor plays,
A laugh awaits in the grumbling haze.

The Dance of Delicate Petals

Petals twirl like dancers bold,
In a garden stage, stories unfold.
Bees with rhythm, buzzing sweet,
Don't step on toes, watch your feet!

A gentle breeze, like a silly tune,
Makes lilies sway beneath the moon.
If flowers could giggle, o my!
They'd tickle the skies, let laughter fly.

Chasing ants that form a line,
Trying to march, oh how divine!
They tumble down, no grace displayed,
In this ballet, no rules obeyed.

So join the garden's merry spree,
Where petals dance in wild glee.
With colors bright and spirits high,
Even the thorns have laughter nigh.

Colors of a Forgotten Dawn

In hues of pink and shades of blue,
A sunrise blushes, curious too.
It shakes the dew and shouts, 'Hooray!'
Yet clouds just yawn, 'Can we delay?'

The sun spills paint across the sky,
While sleepy flowers start to sigh.
A tulip yawns, stretches with flair,
'More sleep!' it sighs, 'Less morning air!'

Daffodils gossip, 'What's the fuss?
Why wake up early to make a rush?'
As sirens call from the garden bed,
They snuggle close, 'Who needs to tread?'

So let the dawn chuckle and bloom,
With laughter echoing 'round each room.
Colors bright, yet dreams hold sway,
In garden laughter, we'll find our way.

Beneath the Canopy of Dreams

Under leaves, a world so bright,
Frogs in tuxes, ready for night.
Crickets chirp the tunes of fun,
While shadows play, the day's well done.

Beneath the stars, the garden sleeps,
With silent giggles, secrets it keeps.
A raccoon pranks with a moonlit hat,
Stealing berries, oh look at that!

The owls hoot jokes, wise as can be,
Tickling the air with mystery.
In this wonder where dreams align,
Every creature shares the cosmic sign.

So let us laugh beneath the skies,
With stars that twinkle, oh what a prize!
In this haven where dreams take flight,
The garden whispers, 'Life's pure delight!'

Serenity Among the Hues

In gardens bright, where laughter grows,
A flower with a cheeky pose.
It winks and wiggles without a care,
Telling jokes to the little air.

The bees are buzzing, having a ball,
As petals droop in a colorful sprawl.
The sun giggles with a warm embrace,
While earthworms dance in their happy place.

Daisies giggle at a squirrel's ballet,
While butterflies giggle at their own play.
A rainbow smiles where the raindrops tease,
Nature's canvas painted with ease.

Oh, to revel in this playful land,
Where every sight is simply grand.
In hues of joy, the world we roam,
In this giggling garden, we find our home.

The Dance of Color and Calm

In meadows where the colors twine,
A jester flower sips on sunshine.
With petals flapping, it starts to prance,
Inviting all to join its dance.

The grass can't stop its ticklish sway,
As butterflies join in the play.
'Come, let's spin!' the lilacs cry,
While daisies wink their goofy eye.

The wind, a partner, plays along,
Whispering secrets like a song.
And with each twirl, the blooms convey,
Life's a laugh, come out and play!

A parade of hues, a joyful sight,
In this circus of color, hearts take flight.
With every bloom, and every cheer,
Here's to laughter, forever near!

Blooms of Tranquil Reflection

In a patch of peace, a bloom takes heed,
With petals like laughter, it plants a seed.
"Why so serious?" it quips and jests,
As the quiet pond reflects its quests.

A grasshopper leaps, thinking it's grand,
While the flower grins, "Just take my hand!"
Together they frolic, a stylish pair,
Creating ripples in the cool air.

The frogs join in with silly croaks,
Sharing tales of whimsical folks.
With every splash, a chuckle spreads,
As blossoms laugh at their leafy beds.

In this tranquil spot, where smiles abound,
The echo of giggles is all around.
Nature's humor weaves through the air,
A gentle reminder to always care.

Harmonies of Nature's Cradle

In the cradle of green, the flowers sing,
As the robin chirps of silly things.
"Why do the daisies wear a frown?"
"Because they think they're upside down!"

With a hop and a skip, the bumblebees joke,
As lilies giggle, "It's all a hoax!"
They sway to the symphony of rustling leaves,
Where laughter dances, and joy believes.

A fox sneaks by in a woolly hat,
While a toadstool teases, "Now look at that!"
With every turn, with every twist,
Nature's giggles cannot be missed.

So here in this haven, where whimsy sprawls,
The earth teaches laughter through its gentle calls.
May we all frolic in this vibrant shade,
And cherish the humor that life has made.

Whispers of the Garden Night

In the garden, shadows play,
Whispering secrets in their sway.
A gnome sneezes, and all is still,
While crickets laugh against their will.

Petunias gossip, lilies sing,
Bumblebees buzz and do their fling.
A hedgehog spins in wild delight,
Unruly fun under starlit night.

Frogs debate the price of flies,
While fireflies dance, tiny spies.
A sunbeam giggles from above,
In this garden, all is love.

The moon chuckles at the scene,
As daisies plot to prank the bean.
With laughter rich in nitrogen air,
Even the soil skips without a care.

Petals in the Moonlight

Under moonlit petals gleam,
A tiny snail begins to scheme.
He stretches out his slimy trail,
While tulips watch and raise an ale.

A chipmunk juggles acorns bright,
As daisies dive in pure delight.
With petals flapping all around,
Joyful chaos on the ground.

Moonbeams tickle every leaf,
As bumblebees take a quick break.
A worm hitches a ride on a shoe,
Laughter echoing in the dew.

The night blooms burst with giggling cheer,
As ladybugs twirl without fear.
The garden's secrets softly blend,
In a moonlit dance, they never end.

Embrace of the Verdant Shadows

In shadowed corners, laughter swells,
Where tangled vines weave silly spells.
A squirrel slips on dew-kissed grass,
And all the flowers barely pass.

The onions roll their eyes in jest,
While daffodils take second best.
With roots entwined in playful glee,
They whisper jokes like gossiping bees.

A toad serenades the night sky,
While butterflies pretend to fly.
Grasshoppers bounce, competing for fame,
In this lively, loony game.

The magic blooms in fragrant air,
As petals share their wild affair.
With every chuckle, every sigh,
The green embraces as time goes by.

Secrets Beneath the Blooms

Beneath the blooms, the mischief brews,
As daisies plot their crafty cues.
A mole pulls pranks with dirt and cheer,
While roses gasp and squeal in fear.

The marigolds join in the fray,
With bright attire, they dance and sway.
A startled cat sniffs the delights,
As petals giggle through the nights.

A playful breeze spills tales of yore,
And leaves rush in for tales galore.
With every rustle, secrets fly,
Underneath the twinkling sky.

The garden hums with laughter sweet,
A symphony of light and heat.
Together they weave mischief and fun,
In every corner, the night's not done.

Musing Among the Garden's Fragrance

In the garden where blooms do tease,
A bee buzzes by, landing with ease.
Tickled by petals, he shrugs and sighs,
"I prefer this honey over any pies!"

Hummingbirds dart, in a curious dance,
Chasing their tails, in a floral romance.
They sip from the blossoms, a sweet little game,
In this garden of giggles, they build their fame.

Each flower's a jester, in colors so bright,
Whispering secrets from morning till night.
With laughter and pollen, they play all day,
Making even grumpy old weeds laugh, yay!

So stop for a moment, let joy be your guide,
Among the petunias, let laughter abide.
For in every petal, a chuckle you'll find,
In this floral circus, leave your cares behind.

Meditations in the Blooming Light

Under the sun, dandelions sway,
"I'm not a weed!" they shout every day.
With a puff and a giggle, they scatter the seeds,
Planting new jokes wherever there's needs.

The daisies debate who's the prettiest bloom,
While tulips perform in their best spring costume.
With colors that clash, like a circus parade,
They dance in the breeze, none of them dismayed.

Sunflowers tower, with heads held high,
"Why did the garden quit?" they cry,
"Too many thyme jokes, it couldn't stand tall!"
And laughter erupted, echoing their call.

So let us unite, in this patch of delight,
With petals for pillows, and laughter in sight.
In the sunshine of life, let's find our own fun,
And bloom into laughter, until the day's done.

Whispers of Petals

In the shade of the vines, where shadows play,
A busy aunt ant trips on a leafy display.
"Watch your step!" she yells with a laugh,
"I'm not dressed for this, just wanted a snack!"

Roses blushing, with cheeks all aglow,
Gossip about weeds who put on a show.
"Do you think," they giggle, "they'll try and outshine?
With their roots all tangled, is that really fine?"

Petals chatter softly, in the green, hushed air,
"Why don't gardeners listen? We bloom with such flair!"
And amidst all the banter, the laughter does flow,
As colors collide in a bright, happy show.

So come join the fun, in this garden of cheer,
Where flowers and humor are always near.
With giggles and whispers, they celebrate life,
Bringing joy to the world, banishing strife.

Garden of Gentle Shadows

In a nook of the garden where shadows do play,
A mischievous gnome stirs up trouble all day.
"Watch out for my pranks!" he whispers and grins,
As butterflies dodge his jokes with their spins.

The mushrooms all chuckle, sharing a joke,
As crickets compose tunes, not one of them broke.
A ladybug laughs, "It's all in good fun,
In the garden of shadows, we dance in the sun!"

Beneath leafy arches, where sunbeams sneak in,
The flowers all wink, inviting you to grin.
"Join us for laughter, let's weave this delight,
In whispers of petals, the world's feeling right!"

So revel in whimsy, where mischief is sweet,
In this garden of shadows, let joy be your treat.
With blooms telling tales that make spirits soar,
The laughter of nature is forever in store.

The Garden's Heartbeat

In the garden where flowers laugh,
A bee took a tumble, a comical gaffe.
The daisies chuckled, the roses all sighed,
As the sunflower teetered, barely survived.

Butterflies danced in a whimsical play,
A grasshopper joined, hopping his way.
They teased a tomato for blushing so red,
"Stop looking so ripe or you'll end up on bread!"

With petals like giggles, they fluttered about,
While a snail on a mission just couldn't find out.
"What's the rush?" he pondered, sliding so slow,
The garden erupted in a jovial show.

So here in the plot where hilarity flows,
Life's little mischief with friends always grows.
Laughter blooms brightly in sunlight's embrace,
In this patch of delight, there's no better place.

Moments in Botanical Serenity

A daffodil sneezed, oh what a surprise,
The tulip next door nearly rolled on her sides.
"Don't catch my pollen!" the iris did plea,
As laughter rang out from each leaf of the tree.

In a quiet corner, a cactus had dreams,
To join in the fun with all life's little schemes.
But prickle by prickle, he sat by himself,
Watching the blooms dance like toys on a shelf.

Frogs croaked the rhythm, a silly ballet,
While ladybugs twirled, a spirited display.
"Oh, where's my partner?" a lilac did cry,
As roses just giggled, too bashful to fly.

Each petal a pun, in this garden so grand,
Where nature's own jesters all take a stand.
Life's not meant serious; it sprouts in the cheek,
In this botanical bliss, we're all just unique.

Tidal Hues of Ensconced Bliss

A wave crashes softly on pebbles and sand,
Where kelp does a jig, nothing quite planned.
Seashells giggle as they roll in the breeze,
While crabs play cards, as cool as you please.

The starfish, it stretches, plays games with the tide,
"Come join in the fun!" they all seem to chide.
One octopus shyly peeks out from his lair,
"Not so fast, my friends, I'll mess up your hair!"

The water's great mirror reflects all the jest,
As laughter bubbles forth, none can resist the test.
A seagull squawks jokes from high up in the sky,
While fish in formation just can't help but fly.

So here in the waves, adorned with delight,
Life splashes joyfully, morning till night.
With currents of humor that tickle the soul,
In the vast open ocean, we're all part of the whole.

Blooming Amidst Stillness

In stillness there blooms a curious scene,
A rogue little sprout plays the role of a queen.
With petals a-messing on silky soft grass,
She calls to the daisies, "Come join for a laugh!"

The violets giggle, they fold up with glee,
As sunlight peeks playfully through each green tree.
"Why be so serious?" the lilacs intone,
When life can be laughter, not grown-up and moan!

The ants form a line, with snacks on their backs,
Wiggling their bums, as they plot little hacks.
"Hurry up, friends, we've got food to proclaim!"
In the humor of hustle, there's never the same.

So here in this stillness, where joy takes its stand,
The flora is bustling, life's a merry band.
With petals like giggles and sunshine so bright,
Each moment is precious, a laugh in the light.

Reveries in a Flowered Garden

In a garden full of blooms,
The bees hold raucous meetings,
They dance in funny hats,
And gossip about their seasons.

The daisies lean in close,
Whispering tales of the sun,
While the tulips play charades,
Acting out what they've done.

A ladybug slips and slides,
On a petal with great flair,
The butterflies laugh so hard,
They nearly take to air.

With cheeky ants on parade,
Marching in a line so neat,
They've stolen all the snacks,
From a picnic on the street.

Pastel Dreams under the Sun

In colors bright and bold,
The flowers wear comical frowns,
They sway to and fro,
As the wind jests around.

A sunflower strikes a pose,
With rays that flash like gold,
While poppies crack up laughing,
At a dandelion so old.

The bumblebees buzz in rhyme,
Offering jokes to the breeze,
While ladybugs chuckle softly,
Reading joke books beneath trees.

Petals play hopscotch on days,
When the sunlight shines just right,
And shadows stretch like rubber,
Bringing everyone delight.

The Softness of Verdant Shadows

Under trees of leafy green,
Where whispers curl like smoke,
The squirrels tell tall tales,
Of acorns yanked from oak.

The grasses giggle wildly,
As critters dance about,
Tiny feet make soft sounds,
Like a secret party shout.

A breeze tickles the ferns,
As they sway and laugh aloud,
While mushrooms wear their hats,
Feeling smug and proud.

In twilight's soft embrace,
The glowworms light the way,
As flowers spin wild yarns,
On this charming, silly day.

Murmurs from the Botanic Depths

From the roots that twist and turn,
Comes a whisper of delight,
A potato starts a rumor,
About the veggies' night flight.

The carrots play hide and seek,
With a cabbage wearing shades,
While radishes tell secrets,
In leafy, leafy parades.

The pumpkins start a band,
Strumming with gourd-like cheer,
As herbs sway to the rhythm,
With sage and basil near.

In shadows low and deep,
The soil has tales to share,
Of wild roots laughing loudly,
In the cool, fresh garden air.

A Journey Through Petal-Laden Paths

In a garden of colors, I trip and I tumble,
Where daisies play tricks and the weeds love to grumble.
Butterflies giggle as they flutter around,
Chasing their tails on the colorful ground.

A bee buzzes past with a comical spin,
I wave hello, but it just buzzes in.
It dances on flowers, so sprightly and bright,
While I, in my clumsiness, race after its flight.

The roses throw petals like confetti galore,
I slip on the petals and tumble some more.
The laughter of flowers fills up the square,
Every moment's a joy, no worries, no care.

This journey through petals is silly, you see,
With giggles and stumbles, it's wild and carefree.
Through whimsy and wonder, I'm finding my way,
In a garden of laughter, I'll always stay.

The Tranquil Canvas of Spring

The tulips are chatting, they never stop prattling,
In hues bright and silly, they're wildly battling.
The sky puts on blue with a wink and a grin,
While clouds overhead seem to giggle and spin.

A frog with a top hat hops down the lane,
He trips on a daisy, but won't feel the pain.
With each little leap, he croaks out a tune,
The music of spring, bright as a cartoon.

Lollipop clouds swirl as the sun starts to bake,
The petals are sticky, like a sweetened cake.
In this canvas of colors, with laughter so spry,
Every bump on the road makes me chuckle and sigh.

With paints made of giggles and bright sunny hues,
The garden's a masterpiece in brilliant reviews.
So I dance through the flowers, my heart full of swing,
In this tranquil, comedic, and folly-filled spring.

Lullabies of the Garden

The blossoms are humming a soft, silly tune,
As crickets do ballet beneath the bright moon.
Each petal's a pillow, so fluffy and sweet,
A full-on performance—oh, who'll take a seat?

The sunflowers sway like they're grooving to beats,
With their long, leafy necks, they dance on their feet.
While daisies spin round, looking for a new friend,
In this lullaby garden, the giggles won't end.

A snail with a top coat moves slow, but so proud,
He carries his home like the best of the crowd.
While the ladybugs laugh, flying high with delight,
In a garden where laughter and joy take their flight.

Each whisper of petals, a chuckle so bright,
In this calm little haven, the stars twinkle light.
The lullabies speak of amusement and play,
In these vibrant green gardens, I wish I could stay.

Flourishing Whispers

A chattering blossom sways to and fro,
While the wind joins the party, all gleeful and slow.
The daisies conspire, exchanging their jokes,
While laughing at butterflies dodging from pokes.

Little ants march in a parade through the grass,
With tiny top hats made from bright blades as they pass.
Through giggles and whispers, the secrets unfurl,
In the heart of the garden, life dances and swirls.

Each petal a paper, where stories are writ,
Of ladybugs dreaming and crickets that sit.
The humor in nature is perfectly planned,
As flowers high-five with a giggle and stand.

So I wander the pathways, where laughter's the guide,
In a world filled with joy, where I won't want to hide.
With flourishing whispers that tickle and play,
In this cheerful garden, I'll dance night and day.

The Unseen Embrace of Nature

In gardens where the squirrels parade,
The flowers gossip, unafraid.
A bee buzzes by, a comic reprieve,
While butterflies dance, oh, I believe!

Nature giggles, a secret delight,
While leaves sway gently, quite polite.
A worm does yoga, stretched on a leaf,
As the sun peeks in, sparking disbelief.

Crickets sing songs of comedic flair,
A rabbit hops by, unaware of despair.
With twinges of laughter in every bloom,
The green world is brighter, banishing gloom.

So, let us frolic in this vibrant space,
Where plants and pets share a warm embrace.
In the unseen hugs of nature's play,
Life's a joke with flowers on display!

A Palette of Kindred Spirits

Amid splashes of color, friendships bloom,
With laughs exchanged, we banish gloom.
A daisy winks, a rose sticks out its tongue,
   While violets chuckle, forever young.

The tulips gossip, dressed smart and bright,
   While sunflowers dance, basking in light.
     A pat on the back from an eager fern,
     Every petal's face tells a tale to learn.

The daisies plan quite a funny affair,
   A leapfrog contest, if you dare!
Laughter rings out, a symphony's sound,
   Together we flourish, joy all around.

In this colorful corner, let's make a stand,
Holding hands with the grass, oh so grand.
With each burst of giggles that nature imparts,
We paint our own canvas, each with warm hearts!

Mornings Wrapped in Petal Softness

Soft wisps of morning tickle our noses,
While petals whisper, like delicate roses.
A cheeky bug jives on the dew-kissed grass,
While coffees brew quick, a dance full of sass.

Birds hold a concert, a natural band,
With melodies quirky and stories so grand.
The sun peeks in, with a wink and a grin,
Wrestling the coolness, inviting us in.

Each blossom shakes off its sleepy attire,
A joy-filled chorus, life's playful choir.
Bees in their frenzy, buzzing with cheer,
Welcome the day with no hint of fear.

So rise and embrace this petal-clad morn,
Where laughter and warmth are vividly born.
For in nature's hug, we find our great bliss,
Wrapped tight in her arms, can't let it be missed!

The Guardian of Tender Blooms

In the garden of giggles, blooms take their stand,
Their charming protector, a funny old man.
With a hat made of petals and mulch for a tie,
He loves all the flowers, that's no lie!

He juggles daisies, a sight to behold,
With petals that shimmer, and stories retold.
"Watch out!" he shouts, as a breeze sweeps by,
Petunias tumble, oh my, oh my!

With laughter he waters, his giggles like rain,
While pansies tease with their expressions of pain.
"Who's the funniest bloom?" they all ask,
And he chuckles, a true comic task!

So here in the garden, our guardian stands,
Wielding his trowel with whimsical hands.
For blooms in his care, it's fun beyond measure,
A joyous protector, nature's true treasure!

www.ingramcontent.com/pod-product-compliance
Lightning Source LLC
Chambersburg PA
CBHW071844160426
43209CB00003B/414